Dasha on the Trail

Dasha on the Trail

Cover, book design, and illustrations by Gwynne Margaret Bruck
Project management by Deborah Young
Printed in United States of America

Sunbelt Publications, Inc.
P.O. Box 191126
San Diego, CA 92159-1126
(619) 258-4911, fax: (619) 258-4916
www.sunbeltpublications.com

24 23 22 21   4 3 2 1

ISBN 978-1-941384-63-3

Dedicated to
all of the kind
people who rescue dogs
and
Mission Trails Regional Park

Hello, my name is Dasha. I am a husky-shepherd-boxer-St. Bernard-basenji-Chihuahua with one blue eye and one brown eye. I have keen senses and . . .

I am excellent at finding things.

Darkling Beetle

Fence Lizard

My favorite thing to do is to go on a hike. I discover
so many interesting things. Let me show you.

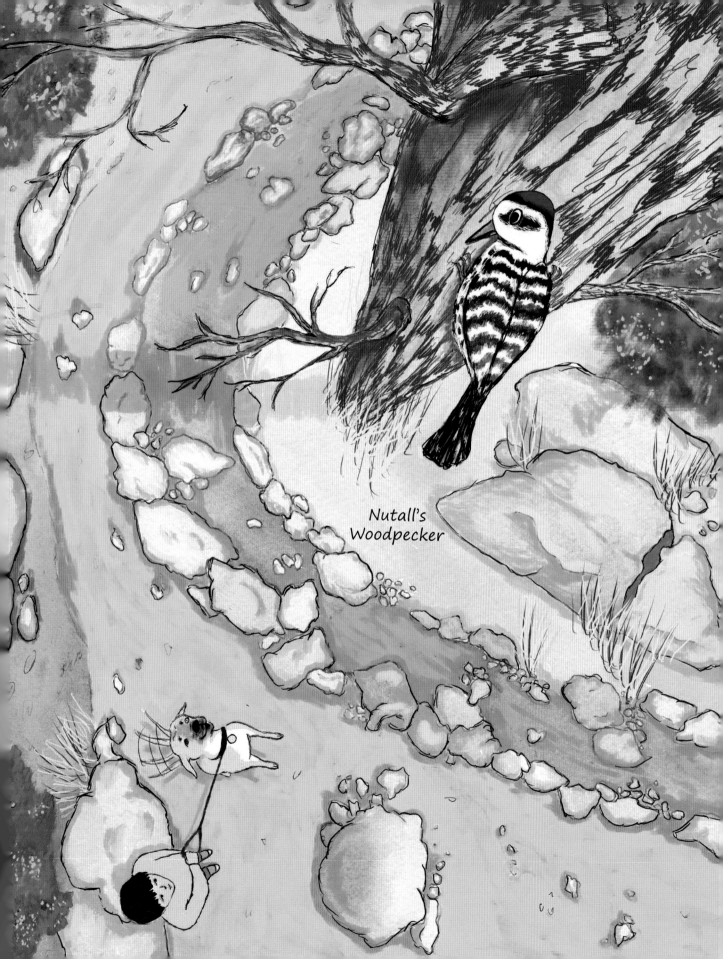

Nutall's
Woodpecker

Dasha loves to hike in San Diego's chaparral amongst desert cottontails and coyotes. There are many parks and preserves in San Diego where chaparral is found.

Balboa Park (trails) – San Diego

Daley Ranch – Escondido

Los Peñasquitos Canyon Preserve – San Diego

Tecolote Canyon Natural Park – San Diego

Tijuana River Valley Regional Park – San Diego

San Elijo Lagoon Ecological Reserve – Cardiff-by-the-Sea

Santa Ysabel Nature Center – Santa Ysabel

Sycamore Canyon/Goodan Ranch – Poway/Lakeside

Today, let's explore Mission Trails Regional Park.

See the raven soaring overhead. If we were
ravens, we would have a view of the entire park.

Raven

Perimeter
Trail

Oak
Canyon
Trail

Shepherd
Pond
Loop

North
Fortuna
Trail

Fortuna
Saddle
Trail

Grasslands
Loop

Kumeyaay
Lake

Rim
Trail

Suycott
Wash

Kwaay
Paay
Peak
Trail

South
Fortuna
Trail

Father
Junipero
Serra
Trail

Mission
Trails
Regional
Park

San
Diego
River
Crossing

Grinding
Rocks
Trail

Climbers
Loop

Visitor
Center
Loop

Oak
Grove
Loop

Pyles
Peak
Trail

Do you know the difference between a raven and a crow?

You can see ravens shrug their shoulders as they call out in low throaty voices. Note their angular tails as they soar high in the sky alone or with their mate. If you are lucky, you may catch an acrobatic air show. Dive bombs, barrel rolls, and they can even fly upside down!

R
A
V
E
N
S

Groink!

24 inches

CROWS

Lively crows flap, flap their wings as they fly. Fan-shaped tails become visible as they land. They are social birds that prefer to gather in a group. They bob their heads as they caw, coo, click, and rattle. Perhaps dogs bark at them hoping to join the party.

17 inches

I'm not a fan of ravens, and I'm not the only one who finds them irritating. Look at the coyotes chase those ravens across the grasslands. The ravens swoop down so the coyotes can nearly catch them. The coyotes leap high into the air but those mischievous birds fly upwards at the last minute, cackling!

I love to see coyotes. They are free. I have to stay on my leash at the park all the time. I'm not as clever as coyotes, especially when it comes to rattlesnakes. The coyotes can live with snakes but I have trouble living with my cat.

RATTLESNAKE EATERS

Give a snake a break!

Why should you leave rattle-snakes alone? Because they have a venomous bite, of course. They have to protect themselves because so many animals in the park want to eat them!

Bobcats

Roadrunners

Hawks

Great
Horned
Owls

Coyotes

101
WAYS
To Cook
a Snake

Humans

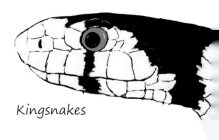

Kingsnakes

Do you know what cats and rattlesnakes have in common?

They both bite when provoked!

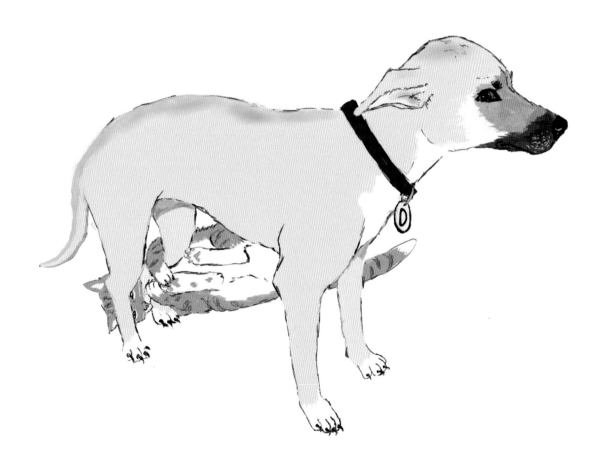

Can you help Dasha
find more animals?

Black Phoebe

Ground Squirrel

Red-tailed Hawk

Botta's Pocket
Gopher

Yellow-Rumped
Warbler

Mule Deer

Striped Racer

Desert Cottontails

So many animals like to hide on the trails but I can find them. My favorite animals to spot are the rabbits. I call this place Rabbit Hill. Here I always see at least one rabbit but most of the time it's more like ten!

Not all animals hide. In the grasslands roadrunners strut right across the trail with lizards in their beaks. They are very bold.

Western Skink

Greater Roadrunner

Ebony
Tarantula

Sometimes tarantulas come out of hiding too. They cross the
trail looking for a mate. At first I thought they were scary,
but when they walk they look like furry windup toys.

How scary is that?

There are so many trails it's hard to choose one. When I try a new trail I find animals, plants, and land that I've never seen before.

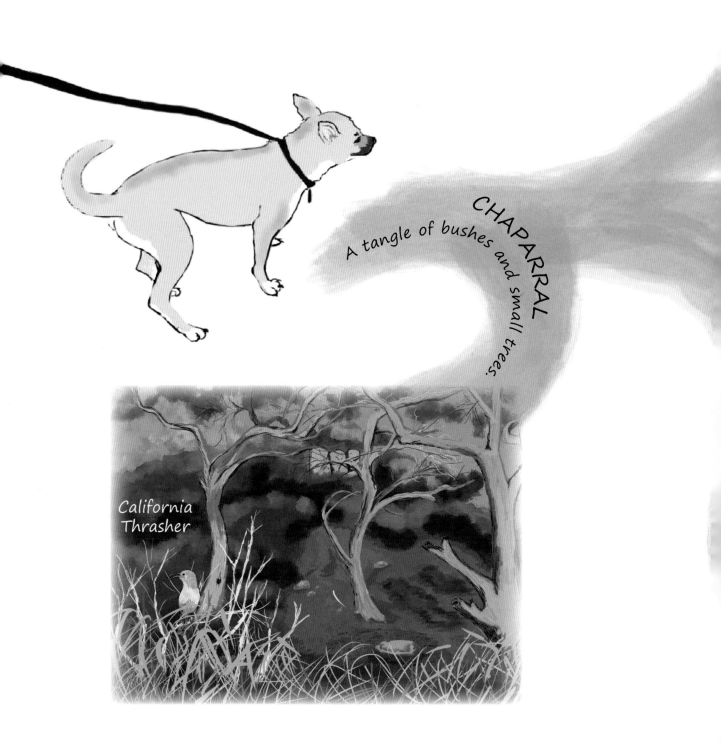

CHAPARRAL

A tangle of bushes and small trees.

California Thrasher

GRASSLANDS
A sea of tall grass.

Raven

COASTAL SAGE SCRUB
A fragrant stroll.

Rosy
Boa

RIPARIAN

A shady walk along the water.

Common
Slider

Coast
Live
Oak

Baja California
Chorus
Frogs

This riparian trail follows a creek. Listen to the frog song under the canopy of trees. Here we will cross the water and climb alongside a rocky waterfall. I used to be afraid to get my feet wet, but now I love to splash right through.

Leave
only paw
prints

We end our hike at the Old Mission Dam which is always bustling with energy. It is a great place to meet other dogs with their families.

I hope I will see you on the trail. If we meet, I'm shy like a rabbit.

Let me come to you, and you may get a lick.